Treble Recorder *from the* Beginning

Teacher's Book

Accompanies New Full-Colour Pupil's Edition

INTRODUCTION

The revision of the original treble tutor book for the new coloured edition has given an opportunity to improve it in several ways. I have changed the order in which some of the notes are introduced, following the successful principles adopted in the descant books whereby the right hand is brought into use much earlier. Whilst retaining the favourite tunes that have helped to make the scheme such an enduring success, there is much new repertoire included — a total of 24 new tunes! Styles vary from classical to Latin American and from folk songs to Scott Joplin.

The extra pages have allowed for more practice and consolidation material at every stage, and there are now 14 duets, of which seven are new.

CD backing tracks are now available with the Pupil's Book, and the exciting and stylish accompaniment tracks will enhance both practice and performance. For each tune there is also a demonstration track played on solo treble recorder. The CDs are a useful aid to the non-specialist teacher and provide a helping hand and encouragement to pupils practising at home!

I find that many people who want to play treble recorder can already play the descant recorder quite well, although some adults do begin on treble. Because of these varied levels of experience I have tried to provide necessary teaching of notation for those that need it, without frustrating those with more musical experience.

Treble Recorder from the Beginning can also be used to teach sopranino recorder, since both are pitched in F and have identical fingering. But remember the treble recorder plays at written pitch, whilst the sopranino sounds an octave higher than the written pitch. The section overleaf on *Using the Accompaniments and Duets* gives some important advice on using the duets with sopraninos.

I hope the revised edition will be enjoyed as much as the original book, and that you will soon have some favourite pieces.

John Pitts, 2008

USING THE ACCOMPANIMENTS AND DUETS

Compact Disc (CD)

Many players will find the Pupil Book's optional CDs both useful and convenient. For each tune in turn there is a demonstration track played by unaccompanied recorder, followed by a stylish and exciting accompaniment track. Here the music is arranged so that the tune can still be heard by recorder players playing along with the CD. The accompanied version always begins with the introduction as it appears in the Teacher's Book.

The CD accompaniment enhances even the most simple tune, transforming it into a satisfying piece of music. Even good piano accompanists will find it useful on occasion to be released from the keyboard and be able to pay more attention to the recorder players!

The Piano Part

The piano introductions set the speed and character of the tune, so remember this when you play them! They lead straight into the tune, so do not stop or slow down between the introduction and tune. Familiarise the recorder players with the sound of the introduction and practise their entry two or three times, counting aloud the beats of the bar preceding their entry.

Use Of Guitar

Guitar chords usually follow the exact harmony of the piano accompaniment. On the few occasions when the harmony is complex, less experienced guitarists may choose to simplify the chords, e.g. G7 instead of G9, and to omit any extra notes added to the chord indications e.g. play G7 instead of G7sus4. Similarly, where the chord symbol incorporates the bass note (e.g. G/C), the bass note may be omitted.

Duets

The book includes 14 duets and of these, nine are for trebles only. The other five duets are for descant with treble, and include three popular items for which the descant part also appears in *Book 2* of the descant series *Recorder from the Beginning* (Pokare Kare; Cossack Dance; Ade, zur guten Nacht). Details are given where appropriate.

Solo or Duet

In the duets for **treble** recorders, the music is arranged with the tune in the top part all the way through so can be played **solo**. But when played as a **duet** it is suggested that the players change parts at appropriate places, e.g. where a section is repeated, so that each player plays the tune. Sometimes the second recorder part has equal interest to the first anyway, so this is not necessary!

Sopranino Recorder

This book can be used to teach sopranino recorder as well as treble recorder, since both are pitched in F and use similar fingering. For the duets arranged for two treble recorders, two sopraninos can be substituted, one for each voice. But remember that the sopranino is pitched higher than the treble recorder, so where only one sopranino is replacing a treble, the sopranino must play the top part (Voice 1) all the time.

In the duets arranged for descant and treble recorders, it is not possible to substitute sopranino for either of the other two recorders.

Contents

Mac The Bark

©John Pitts 2008

Using notes E D and C

All of the first tunes in the book use only three notes: E D and C.

The Pupil's Book explains how to play these notes.

Make sure the players hold their recorders correctly, with the LEFT hand above the right hand. Do be insistent about this, as it is very difficult to persuade new players to change their hands round later!

When fingers of either hand are not in use they are held directly above their own holes, about 2cms away, ready for use. The right thumb is only used to support the recorder and is placed at the back, between right-hand fingers 1 and 2 (R1 and R2). Keep the right thumb placed here to support the instrument, even when the right-hand fingers are not being used.

Finger holes are covered by the pads of the fingers, not the fingertips.

Traffic Warden

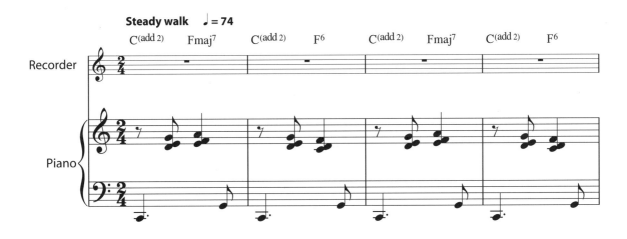

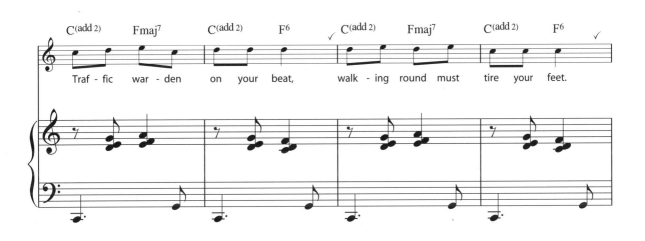

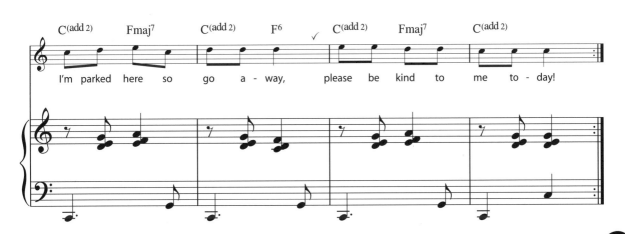

Who's That Yonder? Spiritual

Who's that yon - der

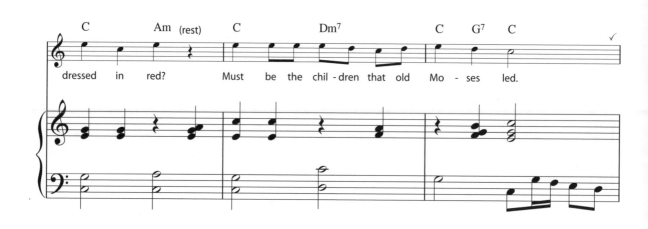

dressed in red? Must be the chil - dren that old Mo - ses led.

Who's that yon - der dressed in white? Must be the chil - dren of the Is - rael - ite.

Merrily We Roll Along Traditional

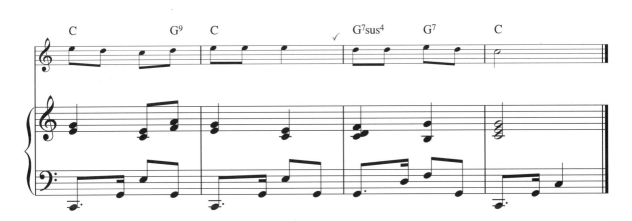

Micro Waltz

©John Pitts 2008

For his last birth – day my Mum bought my Dad a lap – top.

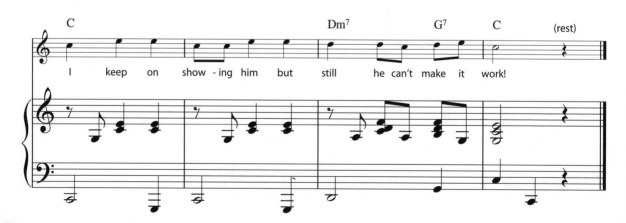

I keep on show – ing him but still he can't make it work!

Waterloo Bridge

©John Pitts 2008

Dinosaur Stomp

©John Pitts 2008

Duet: tune with ostinato accompaniment

When the recorders can play this tune well, divide into two groups. One group can play 'down to the swamp' (the last bar of the first line in the Pupil's Book) again and again whilst the other group plays the tune.

This is called an **ostinato** accompaniment. Let the ostinato players start first and play the ostinato twice before the others join in with the tune. This arrangement will fit with the piano or CD accompaniment.

At the end of the piece let the players change parts and repeat the introduction and tune.

Millennium Galliard

NB See pages 14-15 for Millennium Pavan.

Millennium Pavan

John Pitts 2008

NB See page 13 for Millennium Galliard.

To begin count "1 - 2 - 1" and start to play on count 2.

The **pavan** was a court dance of the early 16th century. It was performed in slow solemn movements with dignified gestures. It is usually in slow duple time and was often followed by the contrasting **galliard** in quicker triple time. While these dances went out of fashion in the later 16th century, they were perpetuated by the English virginalists as keyboard pieces. Famous composers were William Byrd, John Bull, Orlando Gibbons and John Dowland. Gibbons' piece *Pavan, the Earl of Salisbury* is a particularly famous example.

Give Me That Old Time Religion

Spiritual

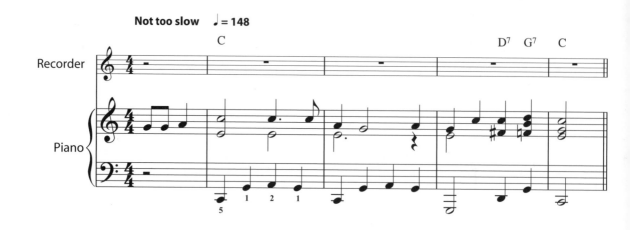

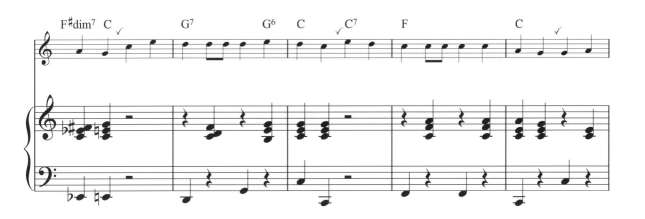

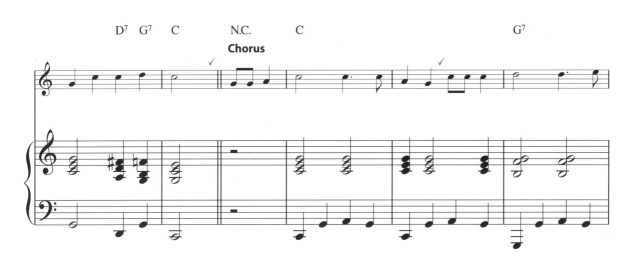

NB The Pupil's Book uses a Da Capo al Fine from the end of the Verse back to the beginning of the Chorus. The music is written out in full here.

Hoe Down

©John Pitts 2008

The Capucine Traditional

Duet or Solo: In this duet the tune is in the top part all the way through, so can be played solo. When played as a duet the players can change parts at the repeat so each plays the tune.

Dance, dance a Ca - pu - ci - ne, Dance round and round with me,

We dance a Ca - pu - ci - ne, Hap - py to - night are we.

French Folk Song Traditional

Duet or Solo: In this duet the tune is in the top part all the way through, so can be played solo. When played as a duet the players can change parts at the repeat so each plays the tune.

Cobbler's Jig Traditional

Ainsley's Rag ©John Pitts 2008

This tune uses a new sign. ⬮ is called a **semibreve** or whole note. It keeps sounding for four beats.
Take care with the tied notes. Have you tried playing along with the CD?

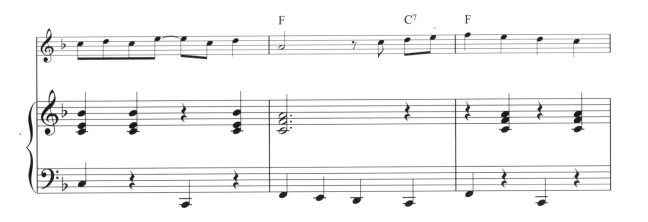

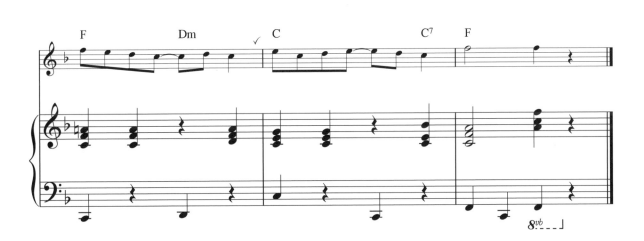

Irish Lullaby Traditional

When The Saints Go Marching In

Traditional

The Pupil's Book has a reminder about tied notes.
Add some tambourine accompaniment.

Tobala Tango ©John Pitts 2008

NB The Pupil's Book uses a Da Capo, despite the Dal Segno needed here.

Two Little Angels Traditional

♩ = 104

Recorder

Piano

Two lit - tle An - gels all dressed in white,

Tried to get to Heav - en on the end of a kite, But the kite string was bro - ken,

Down they both fell, They tried to get to Heav - en but they both went to Hell!

Anglaise G.F. Handel

Judge's Dance Traditional

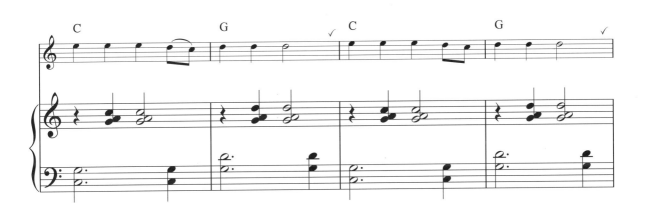

The Pearly Adriatic Traditional

NB The Pupil's Book uses a Da Capo instead of the Dal Segno given here.

Teaching point: At the change of time from $\frac{3}{4}$ to $\frac{2}{4}$, try to keep the crotchet speed the same.
This will automatically give a feeling of greater speed in the $\frac{2}{4}$ section, followed by a return to the more leisurely $\frac{3}{4}$ opening.

The **pause** sign ⌢ : The note (or rest) under this sign must be lengthened. A total length of double the normal value is usually right.

Jingle Bells J. S. Pierpont

This well-known tune introduces two new rhythms.

Suggestions for accompaniment:

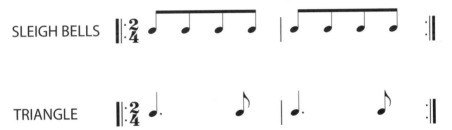

Both instruments can end with a good rattle (trill) on the last note.

Drink To Me Only Traditional

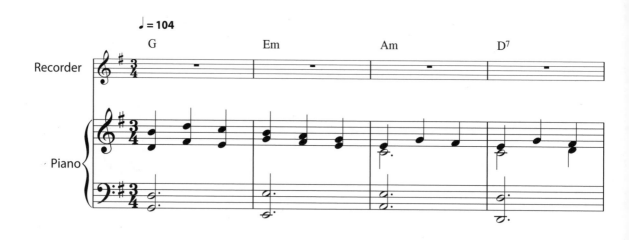

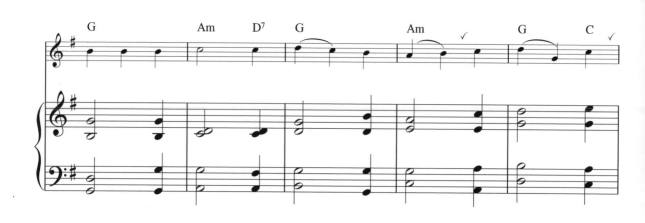

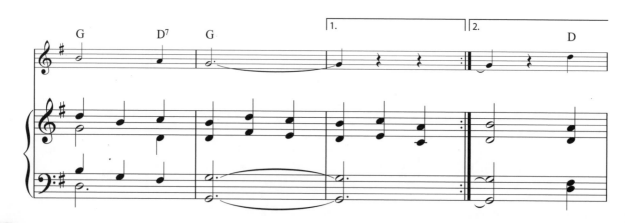

Czech Polka *J. Strauss*

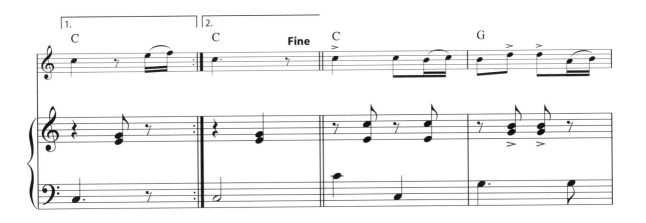

Pokare Kare *Maori Song*

Piano accompaniment: Don't go too quickly! Play with a 'swing', slightly accenting the first beat of each bar.

The descant recorder part of this piece also appears in *Recorder From The Beginning Book 2* by John Pitts, pub. Music Sales Ltd.

Cossack Dance

©John Pitts 2008

NB 2 = optional alternative fingering. See Pupil's Book page 54 for advice on this.

The descant recorder part of this piece also appears in *Recorder From The Beginning Book 2* by John Pitts, pub. Music Sales Ltd.

Michael, Row The Boat Ashore

Traditional

Alouette French Song

He's Got The Whole World In His Hands

Spiritual

NB The Pupil's Book uses a Da Capo, despite the Dal Segno needed here.

Ye Banks And Braes Scottish Air

Rigaudon Chédeville

Duet for TWO TREBLES or Descant and Treble

The **Rigaudon** was a French dance, popular at the court of Louis XIV (1645–1715).

Solo or Duet: The tune is written in the top part all the way through, so can be played by treble solo. When played as a treble duet the players can change parts for the repeat at the end of each section.

Stuart's Boogie

Solo or Duet: The tune is written in the top part all the way through, so can be played solo. When played as a duet the players can change parts at the repeat so that each plays the main tune (which includes note top A!).

Manx Lullaby Traditional

Piano introduction: This uses the second line of the recorder tune, so get the recorder players to follow it in their books.

NB The Pupil's Book uses a Da Capo, despite the Dal Segno needed here.

Sweet Betsy From Pyke American Song

Helston Furry Dance

Cornish Spring Festival Dance

The **Furry Dance** at Helston in Cornwall is an ancient May ceremony which takes place on Furry Day, 8th May, which is also the Feast of St Michael, patron saint of the parish. Furry Day (sometimes called Flora Day) is still a tremendous occasion in Helston, often with over 1,000 dancers taking part in the four dances during the day, and thousands of spectators. The town is decorated with bunting, flowers and greenery.

Jodie's Beguine

©John Pitts 2008

Duet for Treble recorders

Andante Grazioso W. A. Mozart

Dear Liza Traditional

NB The recorder music is written in full with no repeat required.

Optional rhythm accompaniment: using, for example, claves and maracas or guiro.

Minuet H. Purcell

The Gospel Train Spiritual

The gos - pel train is com - ing, I hear it just at hand,_____ I hear the car wheels mov - ing, And

Percussion: A guiro will help to make a good 'train' accompaniment.

Let The Toast Pass scottish

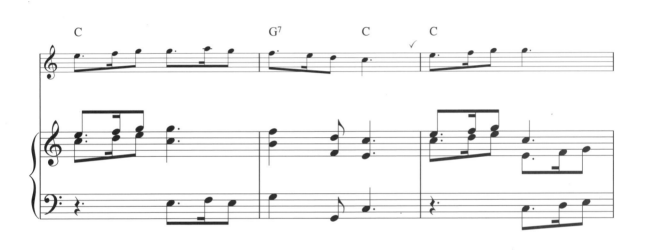

Ade, zur guten Nacht German

Tango Las Pipinas

©John Pitts 2008

Siciliano F. Barsanti

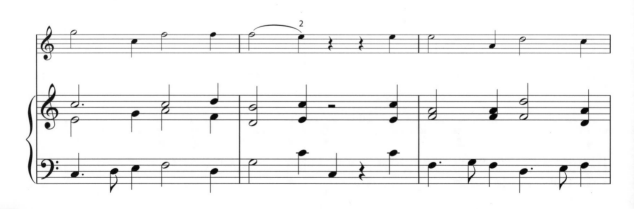

(getting slower)

Blue Monday

Woofenbacker's Rag

©John Pitts 2008

NB The Pupil's Book uses a Da Capo, despite the Dal Segno needed here.

Rigadoon H. Purcell

DUET for Treble recorders

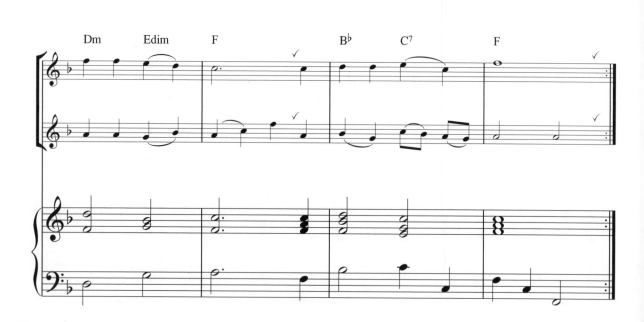

Joshua Fought The Battle Of Jericho

Spiritual

NB The Pupil's Book uses a Da Capo, despite the Dal Segno needed in the piano part.

Play the piece rhythmically and steadily, not too fast.

Cradle Song (Wiegenlied) J. Brahms

The Pupil's Book points out that this piece can be played in two ways:

1. Tune only, for Treble recorders;
2. Duet, for Descant and Treble recorders. Descant recorders play the tune, Trebles play the accompaniment.

Remember that sometimes it is good to have the recorders play a duet *without* piano accompaniment! You might try this here.

Sur le Pont d'Avignon French

Sur le Pont d'A - vig - non l'on - y dan - se, l'on - y dan - se,

Sur le Pont d'A - vig - non, l'on - y dan - se tout en rond. Les

beaux mes - sieurs font comme ci. Les bel - les dames font comme ça.

NB The Pupil's Book uses a Da Capo instead of the Dal Segno given here.

Go Down, Moses Spiritual

Waikaremoana Maori Song

Solo or Duet: You can play this piece in three different ways:

1. Tune only, for Treble solo;
2. Duet for Trebles;
3. Duet for Descant and Trebles. Descants play voice 1.

NB The Pupil's Book uses a Da Capo, despite the Dal Segno needed here.

El Lanero   Venezuelan Cowboy Dance

El Lanero is a joropa, a popular carnival dance. The music is often in a minor key and made up of short sections. The rhythm is syncopated by combining $\frac{3}{4}$ and $\frac{6}{8}$ time, e.g.:

1   2   3   1 - 2 3   4 - 5   6   1 - 2   3   4 - 5   6   1   2 - 3

89

Annie Laurie Scottish

Minuet G. F. Handel

Air in D minor H. Purcell

O Sole Mio Music by Eduardo di Capua (arr. John Pitts)

Weeping Willow Scott Joplin

A Ragtime Two Step

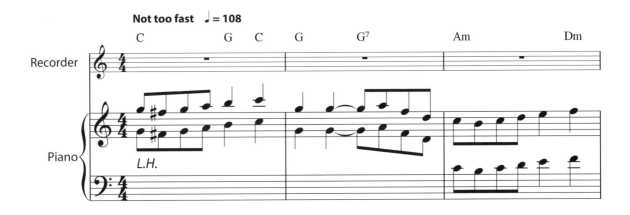

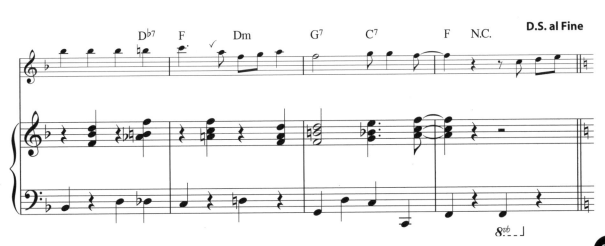

Ecossaise Beethoven

Gavotte G. F. Handel

Solo or Duet: The tune is written in the top part all the way through, so can be played solo. When played as a duet, notice that the music for the 2nd part often copies the 1st, and has lots of interest.

The **gavotte** is a rather dignified French dance (though not slow) that was popular at the court of King Louis XIV. It was also often used in 18th-century keyboard suites, which were collections of dances to play for listening and enjoyment.

Published by
Chester Music Limited
part of The Music Sales Group.

Exclusive Distributors:
Music Sales Limited
Distribution Centre, Newmarket Road, Bury St Edmunds,
Suffolk, IP33 3YB, UK.

Music Sales Corporation
257 Park Avenue South, New York, NY10010,
United States of America.

Music Sales Pty Limited
20 Resolution Drive, Caringbah, NSW 2229, Australia.

Order No. CH73854
ISBN 978-1-84772-678-0
© Copyright 1983, 2008 John Pitts.
First published in 1983 E.J. Arnold & Sons Limited.
Published in 1990 by Thomas Nelson & Sons Limited.
Published in 1995 by Music Sales Limited.
This edition published in 2008 by Chester Music Limited,
14-15 Berners Street, London W1T 3LJ.

Edited by Rachel Payne.
Engraving and layout by Camden Music.

Printed in the EU.